T0354836

STORIES TO TELL

JORDAN A. JEFFERSON

authorHOUSE

AuthorHouse™
1663 Liberty Drive
Bloomington, IN 47403
www.authorhouse.com
Phone: 1 (800) 839-8640

Published by AuthorHouse 03/03/2020

ISBN: 978-1-7283-4983-1 (sc)
ISBN: 978-1-7283-4982-4 (e)

Print information available on the last page.

CONTENTS

Killer.. 1

Strong Stomach.. 3

Bill... 5

The Bear.. 7

The Bear 2... 9

Soldier Hamster 11

Shaolin Goose 13

Abbot Crane 17

Shaolin Ostrich 21

Wooden Elephant 25

The Basketball Rabbit 27

Abbot Cat 29

Boss Dog.. 31

Fearless Dog... 35

Kung fu white cat.. 37

Kung Fu White Hamster 41

KILLER

On September eleventh 2001 Osama Ben Laden bombed the twin towers. Fast forward years later, George Zimmerman followed a young boy named Treyvonne Martin home and murdered him in cold blood. Murders happen all the time in the United States of America. The United States is notorious for having the biggest guns and the most murders shown on the news. It would always hurt me to turn on the news and see another killing happen on the news. Guns originally came from rockets being used in China, but our country was found by a nation of criminals. Still murderers continue to prevail. I don't care who you are, going to prison will make you feel like a goldfish trapped in a shark tank. In today's time, the murder rate has gone up. Nobody really in this world wants to die. Most murders that happen in the news are often over drugs or over a woman. So to all children across the world follow your dreams and don't become a killer because if you end up in prison they will break you.

STRONG STOMACH

There once was a man that played football and was really good at it as well. He could eat anything that didn't move. Well once he realized this along, with him working out his body so much, he later developed powers from a powerful goddess that rubbed his stomach. Then he could even eat laxatives (some times even poison) and nothing happened to him at all. Sure he loved delicious food but no matter how nasty it was he could eat it as long as it did not move and digest it and absolutely nothing happened to him at all. Along with the fact that he was born so poor nothing can contain this man's hunger. Women naturally fell to their knees knowing this man can digest anything. He ate chitlins, calamari, marlin, and even went on game shows such as Fear Factor and he had no trouble walking away with the grand prize. He even went to China once and ate rats, dogs, cats, monkey's and much more! He even went to Alabama and ate gator. When he was at the Japanese steak house he ate tons of sushi and raw meat. So the moral of this story is find what you love to do and make money off of it.

BILL

There once was a man named Bill. All of the girls where madly in love with Bill and wanted to have his child, especially two girls. One of those girl's name was Sasha and the other girl's name was Katrina. Now mind you, Katrina was from the projects and was very robust, meanwhile Sasha came from a very good suburban home and well to do family, but both wanted this man Bill very badly. Katrina not only had problems in the home but Katrina was very loose and easy. Sasha knew this and was willing to do anything to take Katrina's place. At parties Bill always showed up to meet with Katrina and Sasha knew this. Bill did not love Sasha but he loved Katrina even though she had cheated on him multiple times. Sasha plotted hard to get Katrina out of the way but nothing she did ever worked so Sasha gets it in her head that maybe I can beat Katrina at her own game. Sasha then began to start having sex with a lot of different men. Katrina and Bill did not really care so this disappointed Sasha. Sasha then decided to sleep with Bill's friends only to find out no one really cared. So Sasha then decides to go to Katrina for advice about Bill and Katrina told her I'd prefer you just do nothing. After this Sasha gets infuriated and decides to sleep with random men more. So one night Sasha meets with Bill at a party but this time to make him incredibly jealous but it still never worked. Mind you she wore condoms and had protection but this time it was still too late. Sasha chose to get gangbanged at a party and caught a terrible disease called herpes. At this point Sasha knew her life was over and she was put through extreme pain. Well to make a long story short Bill and Katrina, broke up but now Sasha was unavailable because of this terrible disease. Katrina made fun of Sasha because she had this terrible disease that she could not get rid of even though she used protection. The moral of this story is live your life and there is nothing wrong with waiting until marriage to have sex, because some sexually transmitted diseases are impossible to get rid of. Even if you see one blister on your sexual partner's body do not have a sexual encounter, because that could mean they have herpes. Thank you for reading this short story and have a nice day.

THE BEAR

There is a polar bear know as "The Bear" and he is always happy and nothing ever gets him down. So he has an owner who is an old witch named Polish and he winds up going on adventures looking for riches and treasure and faces evil, villainous ninjas, and many other perilous dangers. The witch named Polish is able to make things happen when he has no ability to take care of things themselves by casting spells and using her magic to remove barriers. How the bear came to be was the witch named Polish casted a spell to turn him in to a humanoid bear after his family was killed and used for rugs and now he is able to walk upright like a human being. When the Bear's family was killed she took him in and raised him but needed a companion. As they go out on adventures he uses his strength and claws to fight off evildoers to protect Polish and save the day. The bear really cherishes Polish because she is the only family that he has left.

The story starts off where their home is invaded by ninjas and Polish is kidnapped meanwhile the bear is a sleep. Then the bear wakes up to fight off the rest of the ninjas with ease and realizes that Polish is gone. This then makes bear go crazy and set out on a hunt to find Polish to rescue her and bring her back home. The evil ninjas wanted Polish bad because of her witchcraft to find out how to cast magical spells to control people and take over the world. As he fights them he realizes that his biggest weapons are his claws and his strength that is what he uses to fight off his villains. Everywhere he goes he ends up fighting more and more ninjas and kills them with ease using his claws and brute strength shattering their bones. He then comes upon a village where he meets a nice young lady that feeds him and gives him nourishment for the trip. This lady's name is Kat. She is completely amazed by him but warns him that the ninjas and how incredibly dangerous they are and to watch out for them because they are sneaky and neither one of them like sneaky people who wear masks such as ninjas. They then become more intimate and had sex because she is attracted to how masculine he is and the fact that he is willing to protect his owner. She then gives him money and the next day he leaves, but on his way out Kat tells the bear "be careful". While he is on the trip it starts snowing and ninjas pop out of everywhere ready to fight. The bear defeats them but this time it is more difficult because it is snowing. He goes into a cave and finds out what the ninjas where protecting gold. There is a lot of gold in the cave so the Bear collects some of it and moves on his way. Then on the way out of the cave The Bear runs into a ninja for hire that refuses to mention his name and the ninja tells him "you are not the strongest, you can not win" and then he walks off, but the bear decides to keep moving to find Polish. Then he comes upon a large lake and has to swim across so he gets in the water and starts swimming but as he gets half away more ninjas get in the water and decides to take him on again so he has no problem fighting them off and defeating them with ease again. Next the bear goes into the mountains and it a thunderstorm starts and the bear gets nervous because it is raining and the bear this time has to fight off a hundred ninjas but even still the bear is not afraid and he takes them on and beats them all. As the bear is walking through the mountains he notices leaves are everywhere so he uses a stick to set off bear traps. Next the bear comes upon a volcanic waist land and fights off five hundred thousand ninjas and beats them all. Then in the volcanic waist land he sees Polish tied up and there is the ninja for hire with a rocket in his hand and the ninja for hire ignites the rockets but the bear jumps out the way and lands punching the ninja in the face and knocking him out. After he dodged the rocket coming at him so he fights the last and final ninja, he beats more ninjas with ease and carriers his owner Polish home on his back. On the way back they stop at Kat's place and have a meal before go home.

THE BEAR 2

The story starts off where Polish is kidnapped and a note is left where she is being held for ransom when the bear returns home with groceries. Thus the Polar Bear must go on another adventure to save Polish and defeat the evil ninjas.

As the Bear is walking up a dirt road five hundred thousand ninjas pop out of no where climbing out of the trees and reappearing out of thin air, but this is no problem for the Bear so he fights them all off and defeats them with ease.

Soon this dirt road leads in to the fiery depths of hell where it is very hot and then The Bear must fight off one hundred million ninjas. As he is fighting them all off the ground then begins to shake. After he defeats them all he then he runs in to a really super thick lady named Katherine after leaving hell in a village who helps point him in the right direction to find Polish. They make love and then the bear leaves on his way.

Then the bear keeps strolling along and an earthquake happens and in the middle of the earthquake another one hundred million ninjas pop out and while the ground is shaking the bear fights them all off. Then the bear finds Polish tied to a tree and unties the old lady and takes her home

SOLDIER HAMSTER

I n Africa there is a house soldier that uses a lot of guns to defend the king and queen as they travel through Africa. The house soldier has guns that shoot rapid fire and a large amount of bullets at one time. His biggest enemy is the regime and rival ethnic groups of Africans that harass tourists and the king and queen to make Africa more corrupt. This hamster comes from a long line of Hamsters that work for the government to protect leaders across the world and the hamster is also a human size Hamster like all the rest of them born in to a lineage ready to protect, fight, and die for world peace.

As the King and Queen escort tourists through Africa they realize that the one woman they hold ransom is a fair skinned lady named Joyce so she gets harassed and the hamster is demanded to shoot the regime on site. Hamster winds up shooting fifty guys are dangerous and armed to the core to protect Joyce, The King, and Queen.

Next they decide to go on a safari and an angry hippo chases their car and rams in to it so Hamster shoots the hippo and puts it out of it's misery.

They come upon rival ethnic groups ready to kill (with jealousy in their hearts and bad intentions) so Hamster shoots up a hundred of these guys and saves the day. "You're not going to get away with this," says one of the members of a rival ethnic group and then Hamster shoots him on site and with ease and there you have it, soldier Hamster saves the day.

SHAOLIN GOOSE

I n the shaolin temple there are birds practicing Kung Fu with all of the other flying monks. One of those birds is a student that is a goose and can really fight. This goose is very aggressive and wants nothing more than to please the abbot. Later on the shaolin realizes it has to go to war with the ninja to protect its way of living and defend our honorable abbot and the shaolin's wealth. This temple is extremely wealthy and ninja want nothing more than to take its wealth and kill the abbot and destroy its Kung Fu and their way of living.

So one day when the shaolin temple is hosting an event showing off their skills a ninja comes out of no where to attack the abbot, but the abbot uses his Kung Fu to make the ninja submit. The goose comes running immediately and asks the abbot are you alright, and the abbot says "I'm fine but I have a strange feeling because we are at war with the ninja, but while we are hosting the ceremony I want to find out who is this ninja, so start questioning him". "Why have you tried to kill my master"? The ninja poisons him-self and dies.

"Go practice your Kung Fu," says the abbot. So the goose leaves with a pair of nun chucks and practices hard. The goose practices his kicks and flips with nun chucks and oh man is he impressive.

Later on the goose is out fetching supplies for the shaolin temple and several ninjas pop out of nowhere to fight him so the goose drops everything and uses his nun chucks to fight off these evil ninja. "Through our Lord Buddha, I am a goose that has evolved in to a humanoid able to exists in the human world and able to beat you". He runs home and tells the abbot of this terrible treachery. The abbot says to all the other birds and monks, "through our great reputation how did you get in to a fight" and the goose replies with "they ambushed me and I had no choice."

Later on the ninjas attack and beat up poor people in the street with out shaolin monks and birds knowing. "The women will be used for prostitution," says one of the evil ninja. Back at the shaolin temple two monks and the goose are practicing their Kung Fu on the steps of shaolin and several ninjas approach them and one says, "I will kill you". With the two monks and the goose they fight off the ninja with ease but feel guilty for using their special technique. The goose and the monks tell the abbot and the abbot says, "Goose if I die you will be the senior shaolin monk and replace me as abbot." The abbot then leaves to search out the ninja and on the road he is attacked by twelve ninjas and defeats them all with ease on his way to find the head ninja, but when he gets there the head ninja denies and lies to the abbot about the attempts on his life. "You are no ordinary monk and you have superb Kung Fu," says the head ninja. "I'll ask you again why have you made attempts on my life" says the abbot? "You are a damn liar," says the head of the ninja clan. Then he bangs his hand on the table. "You of all people should know revenge is a sin," says the head ninja. The abbot nods and walks out because he is disgusted with the ninjas and their anger. "This means war" says the head of the ninja clan, "this means war" as he shouts again. He continues to say this as he walks out.

Meanwhile "all my plans to stop shaolin have failed and I want all of you ninja to attack shaolin at once and end them for good" says the head ninja. That night while all of shaolin are sleeping the ninja attack the shaolin temple and burn it by setting it on fire. The monks and the birds wake up and fight like no other and are able to fight off all of the other ninja in the temple and put out the fire in time while a lot of it has been burned down.

skill like no other while the goose practices the hardest on his nun chucks. They practice so hard that some of the members throw up. "Shaolin is a place for holiness, not a place for killing," says the abbot to everyone else.

The ninja goes back to the head ninja wounded and bruised and the head ninja says "those damn monks will burn in hell if it's the last thing I do!" Well that night a female ninja sneaks in to the goose's bed room and tries to seduce him in his sleep but he wakes up and grabs his nun chucks and fights with her but just as he is about to kill her she says, "Please don't kill me, I was sent here by the head ninja to kill you but you have overpowered me so now you are my new master, please teach me your kung fu skill." He looks close enough and realizes that she is a black girl. She then kneels and says, "I hate the ninja and their wicked treachery!" He nods and accepts her as his student. "Lay with me, if nothing else teach me your skills". He nods, she converts over to Buddhism, and then she is accepted as a student at shaolin. "You are my master says the girl ninja." The next morning the girl ninja educates the shaolin on their ninja techniques and weapons. They all practice very hard and that night the goose is impressed so him and the girl ninja make sweet love." The next day the abbot says, "I do not approve of your student to the goose, she is still not one of us." "Do you love this girl?" says the abbot. "Yes I do." Says the goose. "Besides you know it is a sin to have sex," says the abbot "and you have broken a cardinal rule, but she may come of some use to us." That night the goose is walking around in the dark and another ninja with really great Kung Fu attacks him and they get in to a long fight. The goose eventually wins and overpowers the ninja but is beaten really badly. He slowly walks in to abbots room bruised and beaten and everyone wakes up." "Lord God Buddha in heaven" says the girl ninja. They all nurse the beaten goose back to health. "Lord Buddha" says the Abbot.

The next day all of the ninja show up to fight shaolin and it turns in to a long and tedious battle. The shaolin fights off all of the ninja and win. Even lady ninja helps and destroys many of the ninja. Many of the monks and birds were killed, but shaolin still won. "I'm sorry I doubted her," the abbot says to the goose. "I will have the goose fight the head ninja to prove shaolin's Kung Fu is quite worthy of surviving, but first I must teach you our deadliest secrets."

The next day the goose goes to the ninja head quarters and fights the head ninja and they get in to a long fight because the head ninja's Kung Fu is so good. He then throws a star at him and it slices part of his wing. So the goose pulls out his two nun-chucks and winds up fighting the head ninja. Then in the mists of the battle the goose looses his two nun-chucks and later pushes his hand in to the head ninjas face breaking his nose and he falls to the floor dead. He used a deadly move that was forbidden and the war is finally over, and because of this the ninja are forced to rebuild and start all over. "You have killed", said the Abbot, "and now you will always remember this until the day you die. I forbid you to fight anymore. You can practice kung fu but because you have sinned I forbid you to fight for us any more unless it is absolutely needed."

ABBOT CRANE

There is a Shaolin monk sweeping in one of the most secretive places of Shaolin and it stumbles upon a chest and drops it and an evil demon is unlocked from it and wakes up and kills the monk with its excellent kung fu skill. It then escapes the Shaolin temple killing many of the monks on its way out. The Abbot later realizes this and tells the crane bird humanoid to go out and find the demon to lock him back in the chest to save the world. So the crane sets out looking for the evil demon to stop it and it finds dead bodies everywhere. No matter who faces this deadly demon everyone is killed by his Kung Fu. The crane sees these bodies and realizes it might not be strong enough or able to defeat the evil demon. So it goes back to shaolin and the abbot tells him the story of how a very long time ago the demon was really bad and locked away in a chest to stop it from killing people and to create universal peace among the land but it may already be to late because no one knows how to stop this demon nor how to make another magical chest to lock the demon away.

The demon gets in many fights and continues to kill everyone in site. The crane becomes very worried about how he will stop this evil demon not to mention we don't have the ancient magic to lock the demon in another chest for all eternity. Then the abbot tells the crane that he too was once an Abbot of Shaolin back when shaolin was very corrupt during the rat dynasty and because his Kung Fu was never beaten (the demon had eternal life because of it's black magic) he was locked in a chest to seal him away from the world to prevent all his killing and mutiny.

Then the Abbot assigns the crane a task to start lifting weights to become as strong as the demon to be able to defend him off but he fears it may not be enough because of the demon's magical powers. So then the crane becomes really strong but because of his work out plan no one can tell. He consumes as much protein powder as possible to become as strong as the evil demon but there are still fears in many people's minds.

The demon later gets ambushed and has no problem killing everyone in site with its mystical and magical strong Kung Fu skill powers. Then the demon does the worst thing, raped a young girl and continues to rape young girls pursuing with his killing spree.

The police become very upset with Shaolin and fusses with the Shaolin and the most recent Abbot. "How can you let this happen?" Then the abbot came up with a plan and said "we need to find a black woman whose powers date back to the beginning to destroy this wicked monster because the black woman is the most closely related to God." So the abbot sends the crane to a black woman named Joyce and she told the crane "as long as you believe in the power of God this wicked demon can be destroyed. All of man's magic will not work but if we pray hard enough on the subject we can find a way." The crane was no longer worried and they both prayed together and she said, "a magical tool may not beat this devil but a tool of God will always destroy the devils work." "Come back tomorrow and I will have a solution." So the crane came back in next day She handed him a flute she had created that was used in one of God's temples and she said "play this and God's powers will overwhelm this powerful demon and destroy him for good. The crane took the flute and thanked her and left instantly. The crane then began to hear voices in his head and felt sick but as he would play the flute he felt much better.

The crane later confronted the evil demon Lucifer and they fought each other like no other fight has been fought before. This fight lasted a really long time, but the crane knew he was not worried because he had a secret weapon and after the crane realized his kung fu was not powerful enough he then pulled out the flute and played a beautiful song for the demon. "Shut up" the demon said, but the crane would not stop playing. "Shut up" again the evil demon Lucifer said, but the crane would not stop playing. The ground then began shake. The demon became weaker and weaker and then in an instant the demon went lost its power and exploded in to oblivion and the world was saved. "Thank you god," the crane uttered.

There was finally peace in the land and the world was saved by God's work over the evil killer demon that had been vanquished. There was finally peace all through out the land and this tool of God (which not black magic), eventually saved the world. The flute was then kept away in the shaolin temple in case if black magic ever returned, and held as it's most honorable and most valued weapon over evil. Then the abbot introduced the crane to Joyce's two beautiful sons Josh and Jake where she too had faced abuse from a wicked man, but God showed her a way to get the devil behind her and that is how the flute was created. They had been baptized in the army of the light to not be evil.

Then there was a ceremony honoring Joy and the crane and they celebrated, ate good food and parted ways.

SHAOLIN OSTRICH

In Africa there's an ostrich in the shaolin temple that has really amazing fighting skills and abilities like being able to swim and jumping high. This ostrich was also very strong.

One night the ninja vampires attacked the shaolin temple in Africa and bit the ostrich and many others sucking the life out of them, but the ostrich had amazing fighting abilities and could not be turned in to a vampire because of it's strong African genes. So the ostrich fought off these ninja vampires and overpowered and overwhelmed them that the vampire ninjas where soon killed and destroyed and the rest of them ran off. The ostrich was very good at giving these ninja vampires kicks so the evil ninjas would fall to the floor dead because of it's strength and disappear while their souls floated off in to heaven. This happened every time a vampire was killed. The ostrich soon realized its father, a senior monk, was killed and the ostrich was devastated. Even some of the ostrich's babies where were taken for food in the process. As the evil ninja vampires fought and all died they let out a strange evil wicked noise like a hyena's laugh, which was incredibly scary.

These vampire ninjas wore ski masks and ninja masks to hide their identity but the ostrich could do so much with it's superb fighting ability that the ostrich was deemed the senior monk the next day from the abbot for it's supreme fighting ability (just like his father).

The ostrich knew some of its family had been killed and had to stop these evil ninja vampires. The ostrich knew some how some way God had saved him and gave him a second chance to honor and protect the rest of his family members and the shaolin temple. The rest of the monks that had been turned in to vampires were still lurking in the shaolin temple but when the sun came up they all died because they were not immune to the sun's rays which is the center of the universe and they too let out an evil wicked laugh like hyenas. The ostrich had a friend who he trained with was a shaolin monk who was eye gouged and became blind, but he lived. The ostrich then talked with the abbot and the abbot told him "don't underestimate vampire ninjas, these ninjas are deadly killing machines. "It can take a ninja over a lifetime for them to complete its mission. If you cut off a limb they will keep coming after you" The ostrich knew it had work ahead of him. Then the abbot sent him on a journey thus kicking off the never-ending conflict for the ostrich and the African shaolin temple to stop these evil wicked vampire ninjas and avenge the deaths of his fallen loved ones. So the abbot sent the shaolin ostrich on a mission to stop these evil vampire ninjas from taking over the world and their sneaky behavior and treachery.

The ostrich kept walking and walking and came upon a whorehouse or brothel formally known as a cathouse. There were no cats inside but only prostitutes and this humanoid ostrich walks in and meets a geisha woman who runs the cat house named Levii, but meeting her she seemed kind of nervous, scared, and uncomfortable. Some people where even dying of AIDs inside while others were begging to get in (starved for sex like some people need food). The ostrich walked right in because he had the money to while others could not. As the ostrich walked in, the prostitutes in the cathouse turned in to vampires and he fought them off easily and won but Levii helped him who was not a vampire and she said the evil vampire ninja used her to do there bidding and now she is going to turn the cathouse back in to an orphanage and thanked him. Levii did not have AIDs but she had a very robust and busty body and fell in love with the ostrich's ability to fight so well and in the midst of all this fighting with the vampire prostitutes she fell in love with him and afterwards she fed him and when the sun came up they made love. "Can I come with you" she said and she showed him that she had fighting abilities as well and mentioned she wanted really badly to turn her corrupt cathouse back in to an orphanage again and that he had saved her from becoming a wicked vampire ninja like all the rest of them. So the ostrich allowed this and Levii continued on his journey to help him fight off all the other wicked vampire ninja that lurked in the lands. How the ostrich knew she was telling the truth is because when the sun came up she lived and survived like a human was suppose too do. She even wore a geisha outfit the whole time and was taught the ways of the samurai by her family members who where all killed or turned in to vampires. She was really born an orphan and had nowhere to go.

Soon the ostrich came upon a large river that he had to swim across with Levii riding on his back. When they got to the other side the ostrich said to Levii "I want you to meet somebody" and then he introduced her to his blind friend. "Oh God" she said. She was petrified, but as terrified as she was she knew the ostrich and herself stood a good chance of defeating the evil vampire ninja. Soon the blind monk disappears in to the fog and as the ostrich and Levii are walking along a dirt road several vampire ninjas run up to them and surround them but together they make a hell of a vampire fighting team and defend themselves very well. It was very cloudy so the sun was not out to destroy the ninja vampires.

That night Levii tells the ostrich that she was a princess but somehow became an orphan but doesn't know how and she was pregnant with a child once but had a miscarriage because the child's father was very strong and beat the baby up in the womb and she lost it and then he left her because of it. It was clear to see that Levii's last man was a narcissist. The ostrich then tells her that the ninja vampires killed some of his young and he had a similar problem so they both layed together and made sweet love again that was very passionate by the fire in the wilderness around the tall trees. The next morning she brought back food out of the wilderness and they ate a really good breakfast because of her skills to scavenge and she cooked the food over a mini fireplace and it was delicious and this showed the ostrich that Levii was a really good woman because she wouldn't let her man go hungry.

So they keep traveling and they keep traveling deep in to a desert and that night they run in to a vampire ninja with a vampire bat's face with a chain whip. It continues to spin the chain whip around and around to aim towards the ostrich and the ostrich jumps out the way and lands behind vampire ninja while the chain rope wraps around Levii's neck and brings her to her knees, but in an instant the ostrich kicks the vampire ninja in the back and the vampire ninja falls to the floor dead, and because they did not want to run in to anymore vampire ninjas they decided to wait until morning to continue their journey. Plus Levii was in pain because of her neck. So the next day she rode on his back until she was no longer tired which was for a while.

So they cross the desert in to the savannah and they run in to a drug house formally know as a trap house. There is a lot of loud gangsta rap being played and soldiers with guns everywhere. There are crack fiends everywhere and people needling each other to get their next fix. So they walk in a meet a man named Matumbo who his doing coke and he says, "I know you are looking for the vampire ninja headquarters, but first you have to pay a small fee to find it". So the ostrich pays and he says, "head south, keep going in that direction and the further you go you will find it". So they head south and as they get further south the grass gets taller and taller and there are more exotic plants growing everywhere. So they come along dirt rode and meet a master ninja with long hair and long facial hair and he is not a vampire and this is in broad daylight and he tells them the ninja's secrets of fighting and their weapons.

Well soon they got to the vampire ninja's layer but it was the afternoon so they had to wait a couple of hours and as soon as it got really dark a giant vampire ninja with a hyena's face appear. As they began fighting it would disappear and reappear. So the ostrich got really still and grabbed it out of nowhere and Levii cut its head off with her steal Kitanna. "It is finally over," said Levii. Then they went home and the ostrich was deemed a prince and choice Levii as his wife. They had many babies and lived happily ever after.

WOODEN ELEPHANT

The story starts off where the teenage elephant has flashbacks of a man with a mask killing his father. Fast-forward and he is in a class with the abbot who is strong and shaped like a ball.

"Gather around class, I'm a show how to make it through the hall of the wooden men". As the wooden men are moving he is making it through the hall doing his stances and the he does a flip over one of the wooden men and lands and then smashes one of the wooden men and breaks the tutorial.

"Awe now we are going to have to fix the hall of the wooden men," says one of the monks. "So be it," says the abbot. The elephant watched in amazement. "You can do it too, with enough practice and repetition," the abbot said. That night the elephant is walking around and another one of the monks is drinking wine and shows him a trick. He can do push ups standing up and also he can fall to the floor and lift himself up by his legs. The elephant realizes he can do none of these things. So the elephant keeps walking down in to the dungeon cells and meets a man that is an expert at kung fu but chained to the wall. He refuses to train the lemur because he is not worthy and his father taught him how to fight.

The next day he meets a beautiful older woman that shows him the crane style and how to walk on Vaseline. At first the lemur slips and slides but then he masters it. She then feels bad for him because he has lost his parent so they become intimate.

The next night the elephant steals a loaf of bread and takes it down in to the dungeon to feed the inmate.

"So have you made it through the hall of the wooden men???" says the mysterious man chained to the wall. "No" says the elephant. "Well I can, silly elephant can't even make it through a hallway of a bunch of wooden dolls." The elephant shrugs. "Well alright, well I'm going to teach you; get in this stance since you fed me." So he shows the elephant the stances. So for the next couple of weeks he practices his kung fu day and night to master the hall of the wooden men.

So he masters his kung fu and the elephant is allowed to walk through the hall of the wooden men. He kicks one of the wooden arms out the way, and then he ducks another and drops down to the ground. He then does a few flips and then struggles a little bit but eventually he makes it to the end of the hall. The abbot then congratulates the lemur and sends him off on a journey to find the man that killed his father.

So he gets out in to the world and he looks high and low but there is no trace of the man who killed his father so the elephant starts to give up hope and then runs in to the man that was in the dungeon who trained him at shaolin. They become friends and they do everything together, but everywhere they go people become quite afraid of this man and act petrified to see him. Later on the elephant sees a wanted poster of this man who looks exactly like him and he finally discovers his true name, Betty. So the elephant confronts Betty about this wanted poster and then he attacks him and they get in a fight. "Traitor," yelled out the elephant. Then the abbot shows up and tells him this is the man who killed your father. "Is this true?" said the elephant. He nods, and then they begin their fight but Betty is so strong he injures the elephant and brings him to the ground. "Let me fight him," said the abbot. Then the abbot brings his wrist to Betty's neck and kills him in an instant by breaking his neck and he falls to the floor dead. The End.

THE BASKETBALL RABBIT

There once was a rabbit that could seriously play basketball. He could jump really high and when everyone was on the junior varsity squad he tried out for varsity and made the team. The basketball rabbit had beaten the best of them in their prime. Bill Russell, Michael Jordan, Kobe Bryant, and LeBron James all lost to the basketball rabbit. He soon became the number one draft pick in the entire country. "You where the first rabbit who was even going to make it out of these projects son," said his father. Everywhere he went people told him you are so good you don't even need to go to college, you should just go to the NBA. He had a girlfriend named Lela who tried to talk him out of going to college and she cheated but he was so famous he just dumped her. "This whole world has got me bugged," the rabbit just said. "Do you know where you want to go to college son?" said his father. He finally made his decision, so he decided to go to UNC. UNC stands for the University of North Carolina. Basketball was his life passion but then he realized afterwards when he broke his knee that he wanted to open up a tattoo parlor to show his love for art and that is how he became the famous street legend known as the basketball playing rabbit that almost made it to the NBA.

ABBOT CAT

I n the shaolin temple there is an abbot humanoid cat that can do flips and knows all sorts of martial arts movements and is very strong. Well, one day it watched a cobra and a cat, fight and man was it a very physical fight. Well, eventually the cat won but died from the poisonous cobra venom. This taught the abbot a little bit about fighting and martial arts and then this is how he developed his style. This style is called the cat claw or the tiger claw, which is a very deadly style for anyone man who opposes it. This cat was a Siamese cat the size of humans, and could fight like a shaolin monk who was strong and could flip in the air. The cat's name is Abbok and his only rival was a wild cat that was a Leopard. Abbok and Leopard would compete in all things growing up but as Abbok became the new abbot of shaolin, Leopard betrayed shaolin and disappeared and was formally know as a traitor nation wide. When this happened Abbok started drinking wine everyday. No matter how much wine Abbok would drink he would never become as big or as strong as Leopard. The truth is Leopard wanted Abbok's girl for himself and when he found out she would not leave him Leopard became furious, raped, and killed her. Abbok's girl was named Taylor but I guess all that does not matter now.

Abbok's prize student was a shaolin monk known as Peng and Peng was sent out to find Leopard to retrieve him and put him in prison for the crimes he committed. It seemed like everywhere Peng looked he could not find Leopard so it would cause him to search harder. Ten years had passed and no one knew where Leopard was, how to find him, or how to match against his strength and agility. This humanoid leopard could do it all just like Abbok because they both where raised in shaolin together as twin warriors breaking bricks and doing flips.

So Abbok sends Peng off to find the Leopard and he runs in to a Lynx and gets in a fight with this furious cat and both of them do a lot of jumping around and hand to hand combat all because the Lynx mentions he knows where to find the Leopard. So the shaolin monk, Peng, runs back to the shaolin temple to find Abbok to tell him of Leopard's whereabouts after defeating the Lynx.

When Peng returned home to the shaolin temple another Lynx showed up and killed most of the shaolin monks in the temple because his kung fu was so powerful. So the most promising student Peng and the shaolin abbot Siamese cat Abbok had to fight off this evil Lynx and over time they overpowered it using their ancient and mystical art of kung fu skill. The fight mostly involved a lot of flipping around and jumping in the air until the warriors from shaolin overpowered the Lynx. Then the giant Leopard came to shaolin temple, so they didn't even have to go looking for the Leopard to find him. As he would approach the shaolin temple the ground would shake and he was bigger than ever before. "I heard you've been looking for me", said the Leopard. So the two started fighting and the shaolin warriors kept jumping behind the Leopard and attacking him that way. Eventually in the fight the Leopard makes one powerful blow at Peng and Peng dies, but Abbok continues to jump behind the Leopard and use his famous cat claw and then the Leopard dies. Aft the fight is over, Abbok is alone and he has to rebuild shaolin temple by himself.

BOSS DOG

O nce a father brought his dog to Thailand to work with his family and earn a little money for the family. This dog was a Beagle dog so it did not look like he was tough but he learned to fight in China from his father. The next day the boss was going in on all the workers and the boss was a Doberman because the staff was moving too slow in his ice factory.

Well two days later a fight broke out and the Beagle's family members got beat up and a bunch of guys from Thailand hopped off of buses and brought chains, bats, brass knuckles, and knives. Soon the Pekingese broke it up and beat up all the Thai guys in the area. "Wow I didn't know he was so tough" his family said.

"Holt" said the boss Doberman. "Come with me he said, "I'm going to give you a promotion". "Wow" said the Beagle. Later that day his family seemed jealous of him, but in actuality they were quite proud.

Well, that night a ski-mask ninja broke in their house and one of the Beagle's family members went missing while every one was sleep and no one knew. The next day they searched everywhere for this man but could not find him. They even called the police to make a missing person's report, but the police told them they had to wait twenty for hours before they could begin the search. "This is all your fault, go out and search for your brother", the Beagle's family said to him. So the Beagle kept looking even in a small gambling house and still found nothing. So the Beagle's family called the boss Doberman to let him know their brother was not going to make it in to work at least until they could find him again and the boss Doberman said "don't worry about him he might not come back". So this raised some suspicion.

Then next the Beagle called in a meeting after work to find his brother and he said lets have a drink one day. So they did and the boss Doberman got the Beagle drunk and he passed out. The next day the Beagle woke up to a whore that raped him in his sleep the Beagle ran out of the whorehouse and one of his sisters saw him come out of there in his family so he ran home.

So after the Beagle ran home and sobered up his brother and the sister that saw him come out of the whore house called in another meeting at the boss Doberman's place and this time they mean business. Only this time the boss Doberman was even more agitated, angry, and hostile. "Stop worrying about it, your brother is probably somewhere drunk with women and if you keep bothering me about it something is going to happen". "What is going to happen?" said the Beagle's brother. The boss Doberman would not answer. So the Beagle, his brother, and his adopted sister all left that boss Doberman's house even more worried and this time night fall came and while all of the other brothers where out searching the sister was kidnapped and even though she was adopted they had to find her too.

As it got darker the Beagle went over to the ice factory to search for his two family members and found his dead brother frozen in an icebox. The Beagle was infuriated with rage, then twenty Thai men in ski masks all come out and appear with all types of weapons and the Beagle fought all of them off and won. The next thing that happened was the Beagle ran to the whorehouse to find his sister but ran in to the same whore that he slept with when he was drunk. "The bastards want to turn your sister in to a prostitute like me and get her own cocaine and drugs for her to make money for the boss Doberman. Then the whore snorted a line of cocaine and said "don't you want to stay with me, I can satisfy you and console you for the brother the Doberman killed" and she moved closer to the Beagle, but he left in an instant with rage to find the boss Doberman and fight him to the death. On his way out of the whore house he found his sister dressed up like a whore with cocaine on her nose and she was drugged up. So he took his sister out of there and they returned home.

The next day the Beagle went to the boss Doberman's house to confront him after calling the police. He fought off a lot of ski masks ninjas this time, but they where no trouble because he was so tough.

"You ruined my smuggling business," said the boss Doberman, so they fought and man did they fight hard. The both were jumping around and the boss Doberman could really fight as well, and so after a while the Beagle overpowered the boss Doberman and the police came broke it up and the boss Doberman went to jail and tried and convicted of murder and was sent to prison.

After that the Beagle and his adopted sister got married and had babies and they moved on with their lives, but they could never forget the evil cruel behavior of the boss Doberman.

FEARLESS DOG

I n China there is a fearless Pekingese puppy whose father taught him how to fight. Well one day when they are out his father signs a death waver to fight in a match but loses intentionally so he won't kill his opponent. Then the opponent's son makes fun of the Pekingese puppy because his father lost the match and beats him up. Later he vows never to lose to anyone.

Years later this Pekingese becomes an adult and his kung fu is so great he can't be beaten. No matter who apposes this Pekingese no one can beat him. "There is only one left," said the Pekingese and that one left was a Rottweiler with powerful kung fu skill.

"Sign this death waver," said the Pekingese. So the Rottweiler does. They get in to an almost never ending battle but the Pekingese has so much powerful kung fu that he overpowers the Rottweiler and kills him in a death match. Then the dead Rottweiler's nephew kills his daughter and sends him through frenzy. Then Pekingese kills off the rest of the Rottweiler's family and is forced to go to prison for ten years. When he gets out he is living under a bridge and an old lady finds him and brings him to a blind girl that grooms him and nurses him back to health. The Pekingese and the blind girl soon become intimate and he practices his kung fu and returns home. When the Pekingese gets home he realizes nothing is the same and his old students are not either. The first thing that he does is competing in a tournament his friend offers so that his kung fu skill can be used to make enough money to open up a school. He then opens up the school and competes in a tournament against the Japanese to show the world who's kung fu is the greatest once and for all. He wins the tournament but is poisoned in the middle of it and falls to the floor collapses and dies from drinking tea.

KUNG FU WHITE CAT

I n New York a Chinese man run tests experiments on animals to make them humanoids and he runs it on two, a cat and a panda and it works. The cat finds a Chinese kung fu outfit in dark blue and decides to wear it. They also learn martial arts from this man by watching him late at night practicing. The panda learns the way of the assassin while the cat learns regular kung fu.

Well eventually both the animals escape and become sworn enemies because the panda becomes bad and goes in to hiding meanwhile the cat uses his martial arts skills to protect people. Well what happens next is the cat wants to find its master to stop this evil panda's killing and the assassin's that he has taught in New York. Everywhere the cat goes he has to fight off assassins and succeeds.

Eventually the cat runs in to the panda while returning to his back alley home under a bridge and finds that the panda is ready to fight him and just when it seems like the panda is going to overpower the cat he takes out some pepper spray mace and uses his mace on the panda to stop it. Then the cat flees and retreats in fright. No one knows what happened to the Chinese man that turned the two of them in to humanoids but the search for him continues by the kung fu cat.

KUNG FU WHITE CAT TWO

So the journey continues in New York and the cat has been living off of Chinese food. So the cat meet a war veteran from Vietnam who teaches him more fighting skills and he masters them so this time he is more prepared for the assassins than even before. His daughter even helped and that's when the cat and the veteran's daughter became intimate.

So the assassin Panda sends more of his minions to attack the kung fu cat and this time he fights them off with ease but then in the middle of the fight a sloth bear shows up and the cat has to fight the sloth bear. "The panda has been to the zoo" said the sloth bear and in this moment the cat realizes that the panda has some how made more humanoid bears to fight the kung fu Ferret out of the Chinese man's experiments. The cat then fights the bear by jumping around him by lighting bombs and rockets and then suddenly destroys the sloth bear.

Next a lot more ski mask assassins show up and the cat was able to fight them all off until a really tall, really big grizzly bear showed up. The grizzly bear took one step and landed its foot in a bear trap and that was how the cat was able to subdue the bears and the assassins.

KUNG FU WHITE CAT THREE

Next the cat walks in to a Tae kwon do studio and meets Bruce Lee's daughter Shannon Lee. So she teaches him Tae Kwon do, Judo, Jeet Kun Do, and Jui Jit su, weight lifting, but you couldn't tell from his work out plan and they become intimate.

Well on day when the cat was out it started snowing and a really tall really big polar bear with a bunch of white ninjas came out and attacked the cat. The ferret fought off all of the white ninjas but could not see the polar bear very well because of the ninjas. So the cat ran and the polar bear chased the cat in to an empty basketball gym. The polar bear then started throwing basketballs at the cat and then the cat because of his training was able to dodge them all. Then a really thick samurai girl named Taylor showed up and they both jumped around the polar bear fighting it off, defeating it in an instant. "Hi my name is Taylor, and Bruce Lee's daughter sent me to help you defeat the panda. He has gotten stronger and he is a ninja now." "Wow" said the kung fu cat and then they became intimate and made love.

On their way out the basketball gym they faced like fifty snow ninjas and beat them all. Taylor cut her leg, but they still won and where able to subdue them all.

KUNG FU WHITE CAT FOUR

On a late summer night when it was really hot in New York the man that created these humanoid animals came to the kung fu cat seeking him out. "My name is Kwon and I heard you have been looking for me," said the Chinese man. "Nice to meet you" said the kung fu cat. "We have already met, but what I've come to you to talk about it the panda has gotten real bad, watch out for him".

Soon a hundred ninjas and a black bear showed up and they had to fight them all. The ninjas where easy but it took a special style from Kwon called Jeet Kun Do to beat the black bear but eventually he was subdue.

The next morning the panda showed up eating bamboo like it was a stick of lettuce and the panda pulled out a handgun and shot kwon in the leg, shoulder, and one grazing to the head. The kung fu cat was not scared though he used his martial arts to take the gun from the panda and the cat shot the panda in the stomach and that's how he was able to subdue him.

"Thank you for saving me you truly are my best student" and that is the end of the story

KUNG FU WHITE
HAMSTER

A giant snake shows up in the middle of New York City and the kung fu hamster has to face it. Somehow the giant snake in its destruction of all the buildings and skyscrapers swallows the hamster whole. Inside the snake the kung fu hamster finds two sai daggers poking it and when cut through air they can open portals to other dimensions. The giant snake then spits the kung fu hamster out and the kung fu hamster has two new weapons carrying it on its way out of the snake. Then the snake goes in to the water and disappears under a giant bridge.

Later a strange woman appears to the kung fu humanoid hamster and teaches him all about himself and the snake. Really she is and angel and the hamster was sent here to do god's work while the snake was created by the devil Lucifer to carry out the demon's evil wrath. The angel and the hamster soon became intimate and made love. The next day the angel was gone.

Not even an hour later the giant snake reappears chasing the hamster all through out the city. Then the hamster cut open another dimension out of thin air using the sai daggers and somehow traps the giant snake in another dimension for all eternity.

Printed in the United States
By Bookmasters